KOMBUCHA

KOMBUCHA

RECIPES FOR NATURALLY FERMENTED TEA DRINKS
TO MAKE AT HOME

LOUISE AVERY

Photography by Clare Winfield

RYLAND PETERS & SMALL
LONDON • NEW YORK

LOUISE AVERY is the founder of LA Brewery. The company uses all-natural ingredients to brew health-boosting, sparkling teas. They currently supply Selfridges, Leon, Whole Foods, Planet Organic and a whole host of London-based independent cafés and restaurants. Louise lives with her partner in East London, close to her Suffolk brewery.

CLARE WINFIELD is a photographer specializing in food. Her work has appeared in delicious and Esquire magazines, among other press. For Ryland Peters & Small she has also photographed *My Modern Indian Kitchen*, *My Vegan Travels* and *Two's Company*.

CONTENTS

INTRODUCTION

a complex taste profile with a tart, sweet base, with infused fruits and a lingering fizz. I am unsure as to whether I loved because I was feeling nutritionally drained at the time, or because I love fizzy drinks – I suspect a combination of the two, and I have not looked back since.

On my return to London, I scanned the health food shops for kombucha and I did find some commercial varieties, but I longed for the micro-brewed version I had fallen in love with in New England. As anyone who becomes hooked on rare specialist foods knows, the only option is to start making it yourself! Not only to save money, but also to understand the process.

We are now in a time where it feels important and culturally relevant to understand how our food is made and where it comes from. Additionally, the benefits of eating fermented foods are touted daily in the press. The link between beneficial bacteria and gut health immunity and brain health are now recognised with continued scientific research.

There is good reason for the growing popularity of fermented foods. There is now much concern with over-sterile environments breeding allergies and intolerances rather than protecting us, as was the original intention. It now transpires that the very bacteria we have been seeking to destroy actually help to protect our bodies by supporting our immune systems. The majority of us will be eating at least one form of processed, sterilized food on a regular basis, and so we need to put 'live' foods back into our body to replace all the nutrients and digestive enzymes that it needs.

Personally, I wanted to change my drinking habits as I had started to experience stomach

I was introduced to kombucha on a trip to Vermont in the United States in 2010, when we found it on draft in a cooperative health food store. After some encouragement from my boyfriend, as ironically I do not really enjoy the taste of regular tea, I tested all three of the flavours available. This was the defining moment as they say… It was more than delicious; it had

issues and ulcers are common in my family. I needed an alcohol substitute and something to heal my stomach, liver and immune system.

About a year after that trip to the States, we decided to go on a life-enriching adventure and moved to the Isle of Mull in the inner Hebrides of Scotland. Emotionally and physically worn out by a 9–5 job, I was drawn away from the city and towards the land. I found a job in a weaving mill on an organic farm on the island, which used only native breed Hebridean sheeps' wool and locally sourced plant dyes. At home, my boyfriend and I learned how to make sourdough and foraged for mushrooms and seaweed – inspired by living off the land we filled our diets with local goods and I got serious about fermentation.

I ordered my first SCOBY (see page 13) and followed the instructions on the packet meticulously. My first kombucha was good, but very vinegary, and palatable perhaps only to me. My friends were not quite as excited about it, so I started to experiment with different teas and infusions to create a more appealing brew. And so began a series of labelled bottles hiding in the corner of the room with wild raspberries floating, added fruit juices swirling and herbs infusing within them. I learned very quickly about the perils of over-carbonation and the genuine thrill of watching a bowl of tea fermenting away!

We're back in London now and in recent years I have started to introduce more fermented foods into my diet, such as kimchi and sauerkraut. I have noticed that I no longer suffer from excess irritability or mood swings, equally I no longer feel bloated or get cramps, and I have the energy I need to run my own business.

I ran my first embryonic kombucha business, Lois & The Living Teas, for two years before meeting my current business partners and launching LA Brewery in the Spring of 2017. Lois & The Living Teas allowed me the time to forage and scour seasonal markets so I was able to concoct weekly limited editions, which I would trial in a small group of hand-picked local restaurants and specialist food shops. Those initial two years were invaluable in allowing me to perfect my craft through continual research and development with my first loyal customers.

With the birth of LA Kombucha, my new business partners, William Kendall and Mark Palmer, saw an opportunity to bring kombucha to a much wider audience, while retaining the ethics and craft-brewed methodology of a small business. We built our first craft kombucha brewery in Woodbridge, Suffolk in March 2017, and are currently in the process of building our next scaled up facility on an old airfield, which appeals to my romantic sensibilities.

LA Brewery kombucha is growing nicely and we are now stocked in over 170 shops in the UK, including Selfridges, Leon and Planet Organic, as well as a host of independent foodie shops.

My dream is for kombucha to be recognised as the ultimate alternative to alcohol and over-sweetened soft drinks. I hope that soon it will be widely available in restaurants and bars, on tap and in the fridges, with a loyal following similar to the craft beer industry.

This book is intended to be an enjoyable introduction to the art of brewing kombucha at home, to encourage good health and natural self-healing with some recipes for tasty elixirs.

WHAT IS KOMBUCHA?

Kombucha is a naturally sparkling fermented tea full of probiotics, beneficial enzymes and antioxidants. At home, it needs to undergo an initial (first) fermentation before it can be bottled or flavoured in a second fermentation. The first fermentation is driven by a small, pancake-like culture that is added to the tea, called a 'SCOBY' (see page 13). Known as a health tonic, which, when consumed regularly, helps the body to come into balance and heal itself, kombucha has a distinctive taste, both sweet and tart, with a refreshing lingering fizz. Drinkers often experience a slight natural high, which might be due to its high probiotic content.

The origins of the tonic are mysterious, with several different accounts depending on who you ask. It is commonly believed that kombucha was consumed in China over 2,000 years ago and referred to as the 'tea of immortality' during the Tsin dynasty. Transported west by travellers, it spread across Russia and onwards to Europe and North America.

Kombucha has many other names including 'tea kvass' (from the Russian), 'tea beer', 'the elixir of life' and 'tea fungus' amongst others. One story of the history behind the popular name is that a Korean doctor called 'Kombu' used the special tea to treat the Japanese emperor Inyoko (Ingy), and his name combined with the Chinese word for tea ('cha') gives us 'kombucha'. Nobody knows if this is true but it contributes to the mystery of this wonderful drink.

KOMBUCHA TODAY
Kombucha is now a vastly popular drink in North America and Canada, New Zealand, Australia and Germany, both commercially and with home-brewers. There is a wealth of information online and a huge following despite limited medical research on the health benefits. In a world where we are continually exposed to pollution and heavy metals, and our immune systems are weakened by antibiotics and oral contraceptives, it seems a good idea to turn towards natural cures, such as fermented foods like kombucha, to assist our bodies where we can. Even without the believed health benefits, I think that kombucha is a wholly delicious drink in its own right – one that acts as a natural energy booster at any time of day.

HEALTH BENEFITS OF KOMBUCHA
As I cover the health benefits of kombucha, I think it is important to state that everyone's experience is different and where one person will feel reborn, another may notice no changes.

I feel passionately that it has vastly improved my well-being, by helping with symptoms of anxiety and irritable bowel syndrome (IBS). I suffer fewer colds, my sinuses have cleared and I genuinely feel energetic and level-tempered... most of the time! Common reported health benefits include:

Detoxification Kombucha is known to be a great liver detoxifier, with one study showing a liver cell of a kombucha drinker maintaining its physiology despite being exposed to toxin, meaning that the damage inflicted by the toxin is limited. It is believed that this is due to high antioxidant activity. Kombucha also cleanses the body of heavy metals by absorbing them and processing them through the body. This is one of the reasons it is important to brew in high-quality vessels such as glass jars.

Joint Care Kombucha can assist in preventing and healing joint damage. This could be due to the presence of an analgesic (a pain reliever and an anti-arthritic compound) in the brew.

Digestion & Gut Health High levels of probiotics and enzymes strengthen the gut and ease the digestion process. In extensive tests to treat stomach ulcers and leaky gut syndrome, kombucha is said to be as effective as many of the prescription drugs on the market.

Strengthened Immune System The probiotics, good bacteria and enzymes contained in kombucha actively balance and heal the gut flora, (micro-organisms present in the digestive tract) directly contributing to the improved health of the immune system.

Other accounts I have heard praising the positive effects include the following:

• President Ronald Reagan famously drank kombucha to prevent the spread of his stomach cancer in 1987, dying only in 2004 of natural causes.

• GT Dave, the largest kombucha brewer in the US, started brewing to help his mother through chemotherapy when she was diagnosed with breast cancer. She is now fully recovered and credits her recovery to the tea.

• In the aftermath of the Chernobyl nuclear disaster in the 1980s, a clutch of older ladies were found seemingly resistant to the effects of radiation, when examined by doctors and scientists. The recurring theme was that they all consumed kombucha daily.

INGREDIENTS

As somebody who frequents farmers' markets and enjoys the process of shopping for food locally, I would always recommend using seasonal, ethically sourced and organic ingredients where possible. However, it is not always easy to find organic products and can be prohibitively expensive. The process of brewing kombucha will work using basic tea bags and fruit from your greengrocer – it is purely down to your own preference. Additionally, in winter, there are limited fruit and vegetables available, but the good news is that frozen berries work beautifully for kombucha, releasing both natural flavours and colours into the tonic.

THE TEA
Kombucha can be made from black tea, oolong tea, green tea and white tea – they will all yield wonderful brews. The only types of tea to avoid are those with oils or flavourings added, such as Earl Grey and Lapsang Souchong, which can damage the culture (see page 13) in the first ferment (see page 20), so it is best to add your flavourings and fruit in the second ferment once the culture has been removed. The two recipes from Brooklyn Kombucha on pages 90–91 are a good example.

Black Tea will produce a kombucha with more yeast activity than one made with green teas. Its flavour is strong and earthy, and the yeast gives a depth to the kombucha with a taste profile similar to that of apple cider. The ideal brewing temperature of the water is 100°C (212°F).

Green Tea is usually roasted then dried and will produce a kombucha that sours faster than one

made with black teas. The ideal brewing temperature of the water is 75°C (170°F).

White Tea is the least processed of all teas and will produce a much lighter version of kombucha than other teas, with a more Champagne-like finish. The ideal brewing temperature of the water is 75°C (170°F).

Oolong, Pu-erh & Jasmine Teas are hybrid teas, somewhere between black and green in taste. They all produce delicious kombucha, but I particularly love a jasmine brew. The ideal brewing temperature of the water is 85°C (185°F).

I like to use a blend of both black and green tea to create a sour but full-bodied brew – as black tea is brewed at a hotter temperature, you can steep it in boiling water, then add the green tea to steep once the temperature has dropped. Experimentation is recommended – I personally like to use a ratio of one-third black tea to two-thirds green tea to give a good all-round light kombucha with a wonderful taste profile on its own before any additional flavours are introduced. The lightness of its taste after the first ferment enables you to add flavour easily with the other ingredients listed in the recipes for the secondary ferment.

Caffeine is present in kombucha but in lower quantities than other teas. Most of it (up to 80%) will be released within the first minute of brewing as it is water-soluble, but if you would like to reduce the caffeine significantly, you can pre-steep the tea for 30 seconds before discarding the water and repeat the steep – the tea will still release all of its flavonoids without the caffeine.

THE 'SCOBY' (SYMBIOTIC CULTURE OF BACTERIA & YEAST)

This is the living home for a mixture of bacteria and yeast that ferments sweetened tea, producing kombucha. It is also known as the 'mother' because of its ability to produce another skin (a 'baby') with each ferment. The 'baby' SCOBY can be separated from the original mother after it is 5-mm/¼-inch thick to make another separate SCOBY from which to brew with. The SCOBY colony ferments the tea by eating the sugar and producing enzymes and acids. In a similar way, living bacteria and yeasts are used to make natural ginger beer, kefir, vinegar and sourdough.

I recommend buying a SCOBY from a well-known supplier (see page 94). I have grown my own culture from raw kombucha but it requires lots of patience as it can take up to six weeks. Equally, a SCOBY can be grown from a raw, unflavoured bottle of purchased kombucha, but if there are any additives at all or it has been pasteurized in any way, it will not work. A grown SCOBY from a bottle of flavoured kombucha should never be used to start a new brew either as the sugars from the fruit differ to those preferred by the SCOBY, and this will affect the balance of bacteria. I have found that white tea over time will weaken the SCOBY, so I recommend alternating brewing with green and black teas to keep your culture healthy between brews.

THE SUGAR

It is important to note that the sugar that is added to kombucha is to feed the SCOBY rather than you, and it is an essential part of the fermentation process. It will greatly reduce during the kombucha cycle and very little is left in the finished first ferment brew.

White caster/granulated sugar is an easily digestible sugar source for the SCOBY because it is stripped of minerals and will create a consistent healthy brew. Organic golden caster/granulated sugar works very well also and is my preferred ingredient. Generally, the darker the sugar, the harder it will be for the SCOBY to consume, so, whilst Demerara/turbinado and molasses can work, they are not ideal. It is possible to train your SCOBY to eat darker sugar, but you must start by only using a small quantity mixed in with white and then slowly increase the ratio over a number of cycles to let the culture adjust. Artificial sweeteners should be avoided at all costs as they offer no nutrition for the SCOBY.

I have also experimented with natural sugars, including maple syrup and honey, but I have found that it does not ferment very well and the culture weakens over time. Kombucha fermented with honey is an entirely different drink called 'Jun', which has its own special culture.

THE WATER

Filtered water and spring water are ideal for your brew. Mains water can be used if you evaporate the chlorine as it can damage the SCOBY. One way of treating mains water is to leave it at room temperature for 24 hours (covered with a loose-weave cloth) to allow the chlorine gas to evaporate. Alternatively, boil the water for 15 minutes allowing extra water for evaporation. Purified water is believed not to contain enough minerals to support the culture, but some brewers report success. If you ask me, stick to spring.

EQUIPMENT

A word on equipment: there are no hard and fast rules when it comes to sourcing equipment for brewing at home. You can spend as much or as little as your budget will allow, but I recommend investing in good-quality bottles. The other equipment listed here is useful but not essential.

THE BREWING VESSEL

The ideal home-brewing vessel is a large 2.5-litre/2⅔-quart capacity jar, such as a pickling jar, which will provide you with 2 litres/2 quarts plus ½ cup of kombucha each time for consumption and about an additional 500 ml/2 cups to kick-start your next brew. It should have a wide opening at the top to allow as much air to circulate as possible – a large mixing bowl will also work if no jar is available. Various materials work well – here are a few to recognise:

Glass is the number-one choice material for home-brewing because it is easy to clean and widely available.

Non-leaded Ceramic is a good option if you can find it. There are a huge variety of non-leaded, food-grade, ceramic fermentation vessels available in the States, which work very well for kombucha, but so far I have not found any in the UK.

Plastic can only be used if it is assured as food-grade by the manufacturer.

High-grade Stainless Steel is the usual choice for commercial brewers, but it is an expensive and unnecessary option for the home-brewer.

Crystal should also be avoided due to lead content, which may work its way into the brew.

How to Care for Your Brewing Vessel

You can wash your jar or bowl with washing-up liquid, but it must be thoroughly rinsed ensuring there are no traces of the soap left at all, as this can damage the SCOBY. I often sterilize mine with boiling water as an additional measure. As long as your jar is very clean with no soap residue, there should be no need for sterilization due to the low pH levels of the kombucha which destroy bad bacteria and nasties.

THE COTTON CLOTH

This should be big enough to cover the opening of your jar with a close weave which will allow aerobic fermentation, but will prevent fruit flies, dust and airborne critters from getting in. A thin kitchen cloth or an old t-shirt work well. This should be secured with a rubber band ensuring there are no gaps around the rim of the brewing vessel. Do not use a cheesecloth or muslin – the loose weave will allow fruit flies to enter and breed inside your jar!

THE BOTTLES

I recommend glass swing-top bottles (like Grolsch® beer bottles) due to the ease in which you can check carbonation levels in the secondary ferment. The seal on the swing-top bottles will make a satisfying 'phhfft' sound as it releases the gas from the secondary ferment, indicating when it is time for it to be refrigerated. You can use all types of glass bottles, though, as long as they have an airtight lid.

WARNING Be very aware that glass bottles, which are not built to withstand pressure, will explode if left outside of the fridge without regular pressure release (every 1–2 days) – even Grolsch® bottles will explode if not 'burped' on a regular basis.

Antique Glass often contains lead so should be avoided when bottling live kombucha.

Plastic Bottles should also be avoided. I do not recommend using them for long-term storage as the chemicals from the plastic can leach into the kombucha within.

In the recipes in this book I have used 500-ml/ 17-oz. capacity bottles as your brew can be easily divided by four if you use the whole amount of unflavoured kombucha from the first ferment. There is no limitation to the size if you adjust the recipe accordingly. Most recipes call for being 'topped up' with unflavoured kombucha so you needn't brew the whole amount of unflavoured kombucha with the same flavourings. You could try up to four different recipes to taste alongside each other from the same first fermented unflavoured kombucha.

THE WOODEN SPOON
A wooden spoon is the safest option for any stirring or mixing you need to do involving your kombucha. Inert, safe and strong, it will also work well with any fermentation vessel you have. Avoid metal spoons for the aforementioned lead issue.

A THERMOMETER & PH STRIPS
I did not use either a thermometer or pH strips for the first few years of brewing as I preferred to use my own judgement, but if you prefer extra clarification, you can use a thermometer to check the water temperature is the right heat for the tea you are brewing.

Most home-brewers will use their tastebuds to decide whether their kombucha is ready for bottling; however if you would like additional clarification you can use home-brewers pH strips, which can be ordered easily online (see page 94). The ideal pH range for kombucha that is ready for secondary ferment is 2.8–3.2.

Note The pH levels can drop quite quickly so you should always taste your brew to confirm it is indeed ready for transferring to bottles.

FILTRATION
After a few brews, when you are feeling more confident with your brew and have started to recognise the floating bits in your kombucha as yeast, you have the option of doing a basic filter (although this is by no means necessary and is purely cosmetic). I did not filter for years!

Paper Coffee Filter & Funnel If you do decide that you would like a less cloudy brew, you can pour your fermented tea through a coffee filter placed inside a funnel into your bottles. Depending on the yeast content, it may take a while for the kombucha to drip through, but you will be left with a clear liquid ready for the addition of fruits and herbs in the secondary ferment.

Muslin or Cheesecloth offer a quicker, coarse filtering option resulting in a kombucha that is not as clear as if you had used a coffee filter. You can also use a pair of tights, once washed of any chemical that may be on them from the factory.

Tea Strainers or Sieves can also be used to filter the kombucha before secondary fermentation or before serving.

BOTTLING & STORING

BOTTLE CONDITIONING & SHELF LIFE

I like to leave my kombucha bottled in the fridge for a week or two as, given a little time, the flavour develops and the kombucha really matures into a wonderful dry, fizzy tonic.

Secondary ferments will yield varying shelf lives. Fresh fruit and vegetable kombuchas gain carbonation so quickly that it is wise to consume them within a week before the lids pop open. Flower, herb, spice and tea infusions will last up to 3 months in the fridge depending on the sugar levels within the kombucha. As ever, you will learn the difference with trial and error.

Learning the balance of sugar versus carbonation comes with experience, so the best method in the short-term is to check it regularly until you get a feel for it. You will not harm the kombucha by opening it up to check.

Technically, correctly fermented kombucha does not go bad – but it will gradually turn to vinegar over the period of a year or so. I prefer to drink it within the first few weeks of bottling.

CARBONATION

Once you bottle kombucha, this is your chance to turn the remaining sugar into bubbles. The amount of sugar left in the brew when you bottle it will determine the amount of carbonation that occurs. I recommend using swing-top bottles because you can test the carbonation easily – you will know that fizz is building up by the sound when you spring the top.

If you find your brew is not fizzy enough, then you can add ⅛ teaspoon of sugar per 500 ml/2 cups and allow it to build up carbonation over 3 days. If you release the bottle-top and hear the 'phhfft' then it has been successful, if not, then wait another few days. It can take a few weeks if the yeast content in the brewed kombucha is lower.

Sometimes it takes a few cycles of the unflavoured kombucha-brewing to build up carbonation, but be patient, the yeast is populating and will yield bubbles before long. One trick to build up fizz is to add freshly grated fresh ginger or unsulphered raisins to the bottle.

BREWING KOMBUCHA

To brew kombucha at home, you will first need to brew a sweetened tea and allow it to cool, then add the magic ingredient (the SCOBY), which will ferment the tea into kombucha by eating the sugar using the air that flows around the jar to aid the process. This is known as aerobic (with air) fermentation and is what I refer to in this book as the 'first' fermentation. It produces an unflavoured kombucha.

When you start to use the recipes in this book for flavouring kombucha – what I refer to as 'second' fermentation, you will notice that after bottling with fruit, the remaining sugar in the brew will then turn into carbonation and low levels of alcohol (usually up to 1% ABV depending on how long it remains in the bottle at room temperature). Once refrigerated, this will slow the fermentation process significantly and allow it to remain at the desired taste.

There are many ways and recipes for making kombucha all over the world, but the common principles are that real tea must be used (not herbal) and real sugar is necessary to feed the SCOBY. The recipe on page 20 is just one of many potential methods which I have had success with.

Keep your fermenting kombucha at room temperature and out of direct sunlight. The basic rule is that if you are comfortable in a room, then so is your kombucha.

Note The cooled tea should be used within an 8-hour window to be safe because the tea could start to grow its own bacteria as it cools.

In the UK, I find that the first fermentation of kombucha takes a bit longer than it does in the States because of the cooler climate. In the same way, brewing time differs between summer and winter. I recommend brewing for at least 7 days for the basic Unflavoured Kombucha recipe, but I prefer to leave mine for at least 2 weeks in the summer and 3 weeks in the winter.

When the taste is to your liking, you can either bottle the kombucha, chill and drink it immediately or wait for it to build up fizz in the fridge. To be more scientific, you can use pH strips to test the brew (see page 15) to ensure the kombucha is acidic enough to prevent the growth of potentially harmful bacteria while leaving the beneficial yeasts and healthy bacteria behind. The pH will rise temporarily on the introduction of fruits for your secondary ferment.

CARING FOR THE SCOBY
When you feel like a break from making kombucha, make sure to leave the SCOBY in a comfortable state so that it will remain healthy and not in the fridge or the freezer. Simply make a fresh batch of sweetened tea, let it cool and pop the SCOBY inside. You can leave it like this for 4–6 weeks where it will produce a much more sour kombucha closer to vinegar – this can be used as vinegar in the traditional sense, as starter liquid for new batches or discarded. If you wish to rest the SCOBY for a longer period of time then you must replace the liquid that surrounds it with fresh sweetened tea.

If you have excess baby SCOBYs, you can give them away, use them in your compost, or blend them into a face mask as a toning ingredient. The internet is full of wonderfully creative ideas to use a SCOBY. Occasionally, your brew may get contaminated so watch out for the following:

The Brew Isn't Fermenting if your kombucha is not souring and no new skin is forming on the surface after a week. This means the SCOBY is not healthy or viable and will likely result in mould.

Mould in the form of patches of white, green-blue or black fuzz growing in round shapes on the surface, can enter through contamination or if the SCOBY was not strong enough to ferment the quantity of tea. You should throw away the whole batch of kombucha including the SCOBY if mould forms. It can be confusing when you first discover yeast growths, but these are not mould – yeast tends to form around and underneath the SCOBY whilst mould grows on the surface.

Fruit Flies LOVE kombucha. If you find a colony of fruit flies growing in your kombucha, you must throw the whole batch away along with the SCOBY. They will have entered either when the batch is uncovered or through the weave of the cloth – this is why it is so important to use a close-weave cotton rather than cheesecloth or muslin. As well as being vigilant about keeping your brew covered, you can also set up a fruit fly trap by filling up a glass with 2 cm/¾ inch of apple cider vinegar with a drop of washing-up liquid. They will be attracted by the vinegar and soon drop into the liquid to their demise.

RE-USING A SCOBY

A SCOBY will continue to grow and thicken and can be reused indefinitely as it regenerates with a new layer of bacteria and yeast with each cycle. Each top layer will be paler and creamier in colour. I prefer to use the freshest, whitest layers in my brews and discard the darker, older layers.

Note Black tea will produce a darker SCOBY and green teas a paler SCOBY – both can be used.

To Care for a Resting SCOBY the easiest method is to make a fresh batch of sweetened tea, as you would do in a normal kombucha cycle, covering and leaving it at room temperature. You can leave it for up to 6 weeks like this and it will become a very vinegary kombucha with a much thickened SCOBY. After this time, I recommend removing three-quarters of the liquid and replacing it with fresh sweetened tea. You can either discard the kombucha, or use it as a starter liquid to grow another SCOBY (adding it to fresh sweetened tea in separate jar), or use it as a vinegary ingredient for cooking and adding to salad dressings. Repeat this process every 6 weeks until you are ready to brew kombucha again.

HOW MUCH KOMBUCHA SHOULD I DRINK?

Moderation is the key, especially with a probiotic live beverage that is new to your body and system. It could take time to adjust, depending on the bacteria currently residing in your tummy. A good rule of thumb is to start with 125 ml/ ½ cup per day… if you have any side-effects such as nausea or frequent trips to the bathroom, then halve the amount. If you do this for a week and let your body adjust, you can go on to double it to 250 ml/1 cup the following week. Once you experience no side-effects, you can drink as much as you like – up to 500 ml/2 cups a day is good. Equally, you might like to stop drinking kombucha for a week every few months. While kombucha is hugely medicinal, everything should be consumed in moderation.

UNFLAVOURED KOMBUCHA

This basic recipe for making kombucha can vary depending on the type of tea used and the steep. There is scope for experimentation once you gain confidence. Like anything, learning to brew the exact taste profile you desire takes time.

2–3 teaspoons loose-leaf tea (I like a mixture of black and green) or 4–6 teabags, to taste
160 g/¾ cup caster/granulated sugar
125–200 ml/½–¾ cup unflavoured kombucha (from a previous batch or store-bought) or 30 ml/2 tablespoons distilled white vinegar

1 SCOBY (page 13)
a 2.5-litre/3-quart capacity heatproof brewing jar, sterilized
a tea ball (optional)
a close-weave cotton cloth
pH strips (optional)

MAKES 2 LITRES/
2 QUARTS PLUS ½ CUP

Bring 2 litres/2 quarts plus ½ cup of water to the boil in a stainless-steel pan. Leave the water in the pan or transfer to the heatproof brewing jar, as pictured. If using loose-leaf tea, put it in the tea ball and steep the tea of your choice (see page 10 for brewing temperatures) for 4–8 minutes depending on how strong you like the flavour.

Remove the tea ball or bags and using a wooden spoon, stir the sugar into the still-warm steeped tea to dissolve. Allow to cool completely to room temperature: 22°C (72°F) or less. Cooling the tea is imperative as adding the SCOBY to hot water will damage it.

Add the unflavoured kombucha or distilled white vinegar and with clean hands, gently lower the SCOBY into the cooled, sweetened tea with the paler side facing upwards and any yeasty strands facing towards the bottom.

Cover the jar with the cotton cloth (see page 14) and secure with an elastic band. Set aside at room temperature, out of direct sunlight, for at least 7 days before tasting. You should start to notice a vinegary flavour as the SCOBY eats the sugar. Taste daily and when you find the perfect balance of sweet and sour, it is time to bottle the kombucha ready for the secondary ferment. I often wait 30 days before it is sour enough for my tastebuds, so don't be afraid to leave it longer. Test with pH strips (see page 15) if you want to be certain that it is ready to drink.

Decant into bottles, leaving about a 1-cm/⅜-inch air space at the top, then seal. Refrigerate until ready to use.

THE FINISHED BREW

As it is a living drink, kombucha will often grow a little baby SCOBY at the top of the bottle if left at room temperature for long enough, and sometimes build up strands of yeast and culture in the liquid – this is a good thing as it indicates it is alive and well.

Your bottled kombucha will likely become a veritable lava lamp of activity… this is a good thing too – it means it's alive! Refrigerating kombucha for a couple of days before serving it often causes the yeast to drop to the bottom of the bottle; however if it floats around, this is also normal and is a sign of a happy diverse culture. Most floating and swirling comes as the live cultures attach themselves to the fruit particles. You will find less activity of this sort with herbs and flowers, which contain less sugar.

It is normal for a sediment to settle on the bottom of the bottle. This is made up of tea particles and spent yeast. Additionally once your kombucha is bottled, yeast can form blobs when it clings to fruit particles – this is not mould, it is part of a balanced culture and contributes to the flavour. It can easily be strained out if desired. I personally consume everything in the bottle including the little jellyfish mother and any yeast 'floaters' as they contain so much goodness. This approach is not for everyone, and if you prefer, you can strain the liquid before serving.

TAKING CARE OF YOUR KOMBUCHA
Once bottled, and the fizz has reached the optimum level (usually 2–7 days later depending on sugar and yeast levels), you should store it in the fridge or an alternative very cool dark place, as direct sunlight can affect the drink. The reason for refrigeration is to slow the fermentation process, as the remaining sugar will turn into both low levels of alcohol (up to 2% ABV) and excessive carbonation, potentially resulting in explosion if the top is very tight and not 'burped' on a regular basis (see pages 14–15).

A miniature SCOBY will also appear at the top of the bottle, depending on how long it is left to carbonate unrefrigerated, which you can either consume (I do) or strain away before drinking.

CONTROLLING YEAST
Given time, the yeast will nearly always take over your brew and will give your kombucha a beer-like smell. Your brews will gradually become cloudier and much fizzier, due to rapid yeast production within and around the SCOBY. Learning to balance the bacteria and yeast in your brew takes time but here are a few simple tips:

Add Extra Sour Starter Liquid to the brew. Some brewers keep a brewing vessel alongside their brew which houses over-fermented kombucha, which is used to store spare SCOBYs and used as starter liquid.

Wash the SCOBY in white distilled vinegar and a lot of the yeast will drop right off.

Black Tea tends to produce more yeast, so using a pure green tea for one fermentation with the SCOBY will reduce this.

'Starve the Yeast' – a method suggested by Len Porzio in 'The Balancing Act' (see page 95). Pour about 10 cm/4 inches of fresh unflavoured kombucha into the brewing jar and leave it for 3 weeks before removing the new SCOBY (see

Re-using a SCOBY, page 19). Filter the remaining liquid (ideally with a paper coffee filter), clean and rinse the jar, then return the filtered kombucha to the jar. It will form a new SCOBY over a period of a few weeks. When the new SCOBY is 1.25-cm/½-inch thick, it is ready to use and will now have a much higher ratio of bacteria to yeast.

A NOTE ON SWEETNESS

Some people tell me they find kombucha too sweet. If you are brewing at home, the sweetness is entirely up to you. While the SCOBY needs a minimum of 160 g/¾ cup sugar per 2 litres/2 quarts plus ½ cup of tea to ferment effectively, the length of time you ferment is up to you. The more sugar the SCOBY eats, the more vinegary your brew will become. For good carbonation, you also need to leave a little sweetness in the kombucha before bottling,

and be patient – the sweetness will drop as it ages. It might take a few brews to get to your personal sour–sweet combination, but this is the fun part and a wonderful discussion point for you and fellow brewers.

If you are trying to reduce the sugar in the finished brew and your kombucha tastes vinegary at bottling, the addition of fruit will make a big difference and add the vital sugars needed for carbonation.

BASE OF FRUIT

PEAR & GINGER TEA

One of my favourite times of the year in London is late autumn/fall when our local Saturday farmers' market thrives. There is a man at the market who only sells pears, and at this time he has four different varietals including Bartlett (my favourite), which has a nutty and smooth flavour. The best way to tell if a pear is ripe is to gently squeeze the top at the thinnest point to check for slight softness, as the pear ripens from the inside out.

We often get carried away in our purchases of fruit and veg at the market, and inevitably end up with a stack of overripe produce, so this is a good way to use up the pears that do not last long once they ripen. And the health-boosting ginger root only enhances the blend with its spicy tones balancing out the earthy nutty flavour of the pear.

1 large pear or 2 small pears
a 1-cm/⅜-inch piece of fresh ginger
about 500 ml/2 cups Unflavoured Kombucha (page 20), to top up

a cold-press juicer
1 x 500-ml/17-oz. capacity glass bottle with airtight lid

MAKES 1 BOTTLE
AND SERVES 2-4

Juice the pear and ginger together in the cold-press juicer. It should yield around 100–150 ml/⅓–⅔ cup of juice. Pour into the bottle, top up with unflavoured kombucha leaving a 1-cm/⅜-inch air space at the top, then seal tightly.

Leave the sealed bottle at room temperature, out of direct sunlight, for 1–2 days before testing for carbonation (see page 17). Refrigerate when the taste and fizz are to your liking. Serve cold.

NOTE The sweetness of pears combined with the ginger will cause the kombucha to get extremely fizzy quickly, and I think it tastes the most delicious in the first 2–5 days after bottling when it is still fresh.

BLOOD ORANGEADE

I lived in Rome for many years in my twenties, and every morning between December and May, I would go to the market square in Trastevere and sit by the fountain and order a bright red spremuta ('freshly squeezed blood orange juice') with my morning coffee. Such nostalgia led me to this recipe. I have written two versions of this recipe with different quantities of orange, to allow for drinking immediately as a fresh morning juice or as a bottle-conditioned fizzy drink closer to a sparkling soft drink or evening tipple. The first, here. can be prepared and enjoyed right away!

I've used, Angostura bitters, a botanically infused alcoholic mixture (44.7% ABV), including herbs, spices and gentian, to create a kombucha cocktail. One of our household staples, bitters add a subtle complexity and depth of flavour when added in small quantities. There are many companies that produce alcoholic and non-alcoholic bitters – some are herbal; some are fruity. They are a delicious quick addition to any drink at the last moment.

2 blood oranges
about 2 litres/2 quarts plus
  ½ cup Unflavoured
  Kombucha (page 20),
  to top up
Prosecco or Champagne,
  to top up (optional)

a citrus press or hand juicer

SERVES 4–6

Juice the blood oranges in the press or juicer. It should yield around 200 ml/⅔ cup of juice.

Mix the freshly squeezed blood orange juice with the unflavoured kombucha at a ratio of one-third juice to two-thirds kombucha and drink immediately for a refreshing breakfast drink.

NOTE This can be topped up with Prosecco or Champage to imitate a Bellini or mimosa cocktail. Do this when the kombucha is uncarbonated to prevent it overflowing!

1 blood orange
about 500 ml/2 cups
    Unflavoured Kombucha
    (page 20), to top up
a few drops of Angostura
    bitters, to serve
a twist of orange peel, to
    garnish (optional)

a citrus press or hand juicer
1 x 500-ml/17-oz. capacity glass
    bottle with airtight lid

SERVES 4-6

Juice the blood orange in the press or juicer.
It should yield around 100 ml/generous ⅓ cup
of juice.

Add the freshly squeezed blood orange juice to
the bottle, top up with unflavoured kombucha
leaving a 1-cm/⅜-inch air space at the top, then
seal tightly.

Leave the sealed bottle at room temperature
for 1 day, then refrigerate for up to 1 week
before serving.

Serve cold in ice-filled glasses with a few drops
of Angostura bitters in each glass to add some
additional flavour and depth. Garnish with a
twist of orange peel if you want to.

PINK GRAPEFRUIT & ROSEMARY TEA

Winter can be difficult when you're trying to flavour your home brew with seasonal produce. Although fresh local veg may be in short supply during the winter months, citrus fruits from southern Europe are in season and at their best. I have experimented with all sorts of herbs to mix with the pink grapefruit used here, and I find that rosemary adds that extra bit of sweetness to an otherwise sour brew.

When we lived on the Island of Mull, in the Hebrides, you could always get hold of a few citrus fruits in the winter. Pairing them with fresh rosemary from the garden (rosemary grows year round) kept a little bit of local flavour in our brew.

This recipe works well with all citrus fruits, but fresh cloudy lemonade with natural fizz also works well. Citrus is pretty versatile and so goes well with green or black tea or a blend of the two.

FRESH HERBS come out very strongly in kombucha as the acidity draws out all the natural oils. I recommend using small amounts of herbs and checking the flavour after a couple of days when you test the carbonation, removing the rosemary once the flavour is to your liking.

1 pink grapefruit
1 sprig of fresh
   rosemary
about 500 ml/2 cups
   Unflavoured
   Kombucha (page
   20), to top up

a cold-press juicer
1 x 500-ml/17-oz.
   capacity glass bottle
   with airtight lid

MAKES 1 BOTTLE
AND SERVES 2–4

Juice the pink grapefruit in the cold-press juicer. It should yield around 100 ml/generous ⅓ cup of juice.

Put the rosemary into the bottle. Add the freshly squeezed pink grapefruit juice, top up with unflavoured kombucha leaving a 1-cm/⅜-inch air space at the top then seal tightly.

Leave the sealed bottle at room temperature, out of direct sunlight, for 1–2 days before testing for carbonation (see page 17). Refrigerate when the taste and fizz are to your liking. Serve cold.

CRANBERRY CLEANSE

If like me, you are accustomed to ordering cranberry juice and lime when you are out at a bar with friends, you will be excited by this recipe, which is an enhanced version with additional benefits to boot.

As well as strengthening the immune system and improving stress levels, cranberries are famed for their antioxidants, vitamin C and salicylic acid. They are traditionally used in the natural treatment and prevention of urinary tract infections, and when combined with kombucha, the mixture can be a powerful cleanser. Unsweetened cranberries are sour and dry to the taste, so depending on the sweetness or sourness of your kombucha, you might want to balance this out by adding either a sweetened or unsweetened version of the juice. I do not recommend using fresh cranberries, because they are so very sour.

200 ml/¾ cup cranberry juice
freshly squeezed juice of
½ lime
2 litres/2 quarts plus ½ cup
Unflavoured Kombucha
(page 20), to top up
ice cubes, to serve

4 x 500-ml/17-oz. capacity glass
bottles with airtight lids

MAKES 4 BOTTLES
AND SERVES 8-16

Mix the cranberry juice with the lime juice and divide between the bottles. Top up with unflavoured kombucha leaving a 1-cm/⅜-inch air space at the top, then seal tightly.

Leave the sealed bottles at room temperature, out of direct sunlight, for 2 days before testing for carbonation (see page 17) and refrigerate when the taste and fizz are to your liking. Serve cold over ice.

NOTE As with all kombuchas, it is good to make sure you are drinking lots of water alongside the drink, in order to assist the diuretic effects of the cranberries and kombucha.

CRANBERRIES are also used to treat chronic fatigue syndrome, scurvy (vitamin C deficiency), Type-2 diabetes and pleurisy (inflammation of the tissue that lines lung).

PEAR, CARDAMOM & LIME SOUR

Along with healthy, fresh daytime recipes, I also wanted to create an evening drink which was a viable non-alcoholic cocktail. This is the kombucha equivalent of a whiskey sour. It's a refined drink that will be an instant favourite of guests who like to guess the secret ingredients.

Inspired by south-east Asian flavours of cardamom and lime, it is easy to make at home and offers an intricate taste profile. I usually use Conference or Bartlett pears and give them a good wash but do not peel them. I like the cloudy liquid the skin produces, but if you prefer a milky white juice, then peel the pears prior to juicing.

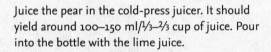

1 large pear or 2 small pears
freshly squeezed juice of ½ lime
1 cardamom pod
a tiny pinch of salt
about 400 ml/1²/₃ cups Unflavoured Kombucha (page 20), to top up

a cold-press juicer
1 x 500-ml/17-oz. capacity glass bottle with airtight lid

MAKES 1 BOTTLE
AND SERVES 2-4

Juice the pear in the cold-press juicer. It should yield around 100–150 ml/¹/₃–²/₃ cup of juice. Pour into the bottle with the lime juice.

Open the cardamom pod, pick out the seeds and add these to the juice. Add the salt and top up with the unflavoured kombucha leaving a 1-cm/ ³/₈-inch air space at the top then seal tightly.

Put the sealed bottle straight into the fridge and allow the cardamom seeds to infuse for 24 hours.

Reawaken the juice the following day by giving the bottle a gentle shake, pour and enjoy.

NOTE I prefer to drink this fresh and uncarbonated when the cardamom flavour is present but not overpowering. You can experiment by leaving it for 2–3 days in the fridge to let the flavours mature and to allow a little carbonation to evolve.

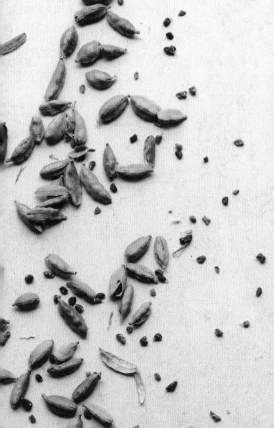

CARDAMOM has its own medicinal uses and is used to ease digestive problems, such as heartburn, nausea and bloating, and as a diuretic to remove waste from the urinary tract, kidneys and bladder. It is used as an aphrodisiac in traditional medicine, an immune system booster and an anti-inflammatory to ease pain and swelling.

CLASSIC RASPBERRY TEA

This was the first kombucha recipe I really loved. The natural tartness of the raspberries complements the tartness of the kombucha with delicious results.

For home brewers, this recipe is one of the simplest. On a larger scale, I have found it to be one of the most difficult recipes to master. In the commercial production of this kombucha, it is tricky to balance the natural fruit sugars and tartness while maintaining the essence and flavour of the fruit. I love making it at home, devoid of such complications, and it always makes me think of summer.

Frozen berries are an extremely good option for flavouring kombucha because they are available all year round. Berries are frozen at the peak of their flavour and juiciness so will pack a punch of flavour that you want to infuse into your drink.

If, however, you are lucky enough to be reading this after picking fresh raspberries from your hedgerow or country garden, then this drink will be a real treat for you.

8 fresh or frozen raspberries
about 500 ml/2 cups
   Unflavoured Kombucha
   (page 20), to top up
fresh mint or basil and a
   lemon wedge, to serve
   (optional)

1 x 500-ml/17-oz. capacity glass
   bottle with airtight lid

MAKES 1 BOTTLE
AND SERVES 2–4

You can either add the raspberries whole to the bottle (I like to do this as they are pretty and easy to strain out to serve) or you can blend the raspberries prior to adding to the bottle. Top up with unflavoured kombucha leaving a 1-cm/ ⅜-inch air space at the top, then seal tightly.

Leave the sealed bottle at room temperature, out of direct sunlight, for 2 days before testing for carbonation (see page 17). When the taste and fizz are to your liking, strain the fruit and re-bottle if desired, then refrigerate.

Alternatively, strain before serving or leave the fruit in. Add fresh mint or basil and a squeeze of lemon for a slight twist on the original.

Serve cold.

POMEGRANATE & LIME FIZZ

Pomegranates, largely grown in the Middle East, are available all year round in local stores and supermarkets. They provide a deep, rich, ruby-red kombucha and a powerful antioxidant punch in cold winter months.

This is one of the only recipes where I recommend using pure 100% pomegranate juice without the seeds, for a rich flavour. The pomegranate also masks the stronger vinegary tones of kombucha, so it's good for 'first timers'. Equally, the kombucha softens the dryness of the full-strength pomegranate juice with the fresh lime, adding a tartness and depth to the drink.

120 ml/½ cup pure pomegranate juice or juice of 1 pomegranate (see method)
¼ fresh lime
about 500 ml/2 cups Unflavoured Kombucha (page 20), to top up

a large square piece of muslin/cheesecloth (optional)
1 x 500-ml/17-oz. capacity glass bottle with airtight lid

MAKES 1 BOTTLE
AND SERVES 2-4

You can either buy pure pomegranate juice or juice it yourself. Carefully remove the seeds over a bowl to catch any that fly out and any juice that trickles away. Put them in a blender and pulse a few times to release the juice before straining through a piece of muslin/cheesecloth or a fine-mesh sieve. It should yield around 120 ml/½ cup of juice.

Add 100 ml/generous ⅓ cup of pomegranate juice to the bottle and squeeze in the juice from the lime quarter. Top up with unflavoured kombucha leaving a 1-cm/⅜-inch air space at the top then seal tightly.

Leave the sealed bottle at room temperature, out of direct sunlight, for 2 days before testing for carbonation (see page 17). Refrigerate when the taste and fizz are to your liking. Serve cold.

POMEGRANATES are famed for containing the highest level of antioxidant compounds of all fruits. Current studies show positive results in boosting immune support as well as reducing blood pressure and inflammation.

STRAWBERRY & BASIL TEA

This is a classic summer drink – perfect for an afternoon or evening non-alcoholic aperitif. The natural sweetness of the strawberries makes it a real winner for those new to the complex flavour profile of kombucha.

Strawberries come into season in Britain in early May and last until the end of July. You can also buy frozen strawberries in the winter so that you can whip this up when in need of a vitamin boost or summery drink to break up the bleak mid-winter.

2 strawberries, tops cut off and halved or quartered
1 large or 2 small fresh basil leaves
about 500 ml/2 cups Unflavoured Kombucha (page 20), to top up

1 x 500-ml/17-oz. capacity glass bottle with airtight lid

MAKES 1 BOTTLE AND SERVES 2–4

Put the strawberry halves or quarters directly into the bottle along with the basil leaf or leaves.

Simply top up with unflavoured kombucha leaving a 1-cm/⅜-inch air space at the top, then seal tightly.

Leave the sealed bottle at room temperature, out of direct sunlight. As strawberries contain a lot of their own natural sugars, this will carbonate quickly, so be sure to check after 2–3 days (see page 17). I like to remove the basil at this point so it doesn't overpower the strawberries. As soon as the fizz is to your liking, refrigerate.

STRAWBERRIES have many health benefits, including fat burning, easing inflammation in the body, promoting bone health with their sources of vitamin K and magnesium and helping to lower cardiovascular disease with high levels of flavonoids. They also possess anti-ageing properties.

BLACKBERRY & APPLE PIE

OK, so this isn't a pie... but it is reminiscent of the warming, hearty combination of hedgerow blackberries and apples that so often find themselves encased and baked in a shortcrust pastry coat, which is comforting in the autumn/fall months. My mother lives in the middle of an apple orchard where she has an overwhelming supply of Bramley, Cox and Russet apples. The tartness and the texture of these apples is uniquely rewarding and nourishing when ripe.

All organic, they fall quickly from the trees to the delight of every flying and earthbound sugar-loving insect and animal around. In a rush, we gather them from the ground and from the trees, before she donates them to her neighbour who rewards her with fresh pink apple juice and cider from his village brewery. The Somerset village she inhabits is surrounded by living hedgerows, bountiful with juicy blackberries, ready to make this brew.

2 medium apples
5 blackberries
about 500 ml/2 cups
    Unflavoured
    Kombucha (page
    20), to top up

a cold-press juicer
1 x 500-ml/17-oz.
    capacity glass bottle
    with airtight lid

MAKES 1 BOTTLE
AND SERVES 2–4

Juice the apples in the cold-press juicer. It should yield around 150 ml/⅔ cup of juice. If you do not have a juicer, you can use store-bought fresh apple juice or slice or blend the apples and pop them directly into the bottle. Add the blackberries whole into the bottle.

Top up with unflavoured kombucha leaving a 1-cm/⅜-inch air space at the top, then seal tightly. The blackberries will dye the liquid purple quickly and efficiently, rewarding you with a pretty cleansing drink.

Leave the sealed bottle at room temperature, out of direct sunlight, for 2 days before testing for carbonation (see page 17). When the taste and fizz are to your liking, strain the fruit and re-bottle if desired, then refrigerate.

Alternatively, strain before serving or just leave the fruit in. Serve cold.

CHIA CHERRYADE

Inspired by G. T. SYNERGY drinks (available in the States), I have come up with a home-brewers version of a health-boosting tonic that you can enjoy at home. Although they create a number of drinks containing chia seeds, my stand-out favourite is the cherry with its tangy, fruity, tart flavour along with the unusual gel-like texture of the seeds that swell up over a short period to a texture similar to pectin used in preserving.

Sweet and tart cherries create a very tasty kombucha, which is wonderful when cherries are in season but equally available all year round using cherry juice.

about 2 litres/2 quarts
   plus ½ cup Unflavoured
   Kombucha (page 20)
1 teaspoon chia seeds
200 ml/¾ cup cherry juice
   or 8 fresh cherries, stoned/
   pitted

4 x 500-ml/17-oz. capacity glass bottles with airtight lids

MAKES 4 BOTTLES
AND SERVES 8–16

Pour 250 ml/1 cup of the unflavoured kombucha into a glass and add the chia seeds. Leave to soak, stirring every 10 minutes, until the mixture has a gel-like consistency. Divide the chia gel between the bottles before adding the cherry juice (or fresh cherries). Top up with the rest of the unflavoured kombucha, leaving a 1-cm/⅜-inch air space at the top, then seal tightly.

Leave the sealed bottles at room temperature, out of direct sunlight, for 2 days before testing for carbonation (see page 17) and refrigerate when the taste and fizz are to your liking.

Serve cold and drink within a week as the sugars in the cherry will accelerate the carbonation.

NOTE If the chia seeds clump together in the bottles, just give them a little stir before serving.

CHIA SEEDS are tiny nutrient powerhouses containing fibre, protein, Omega-3s, calcium, manganese, magnesium, phosphorous, zinc, potassium and vitamins B1, B2 and B3!

BLUEBERRY LEMONADE

On my last trip to Maine in the US, I had a wonderful blueberry kombucha from a local brewery, which inspired me to write this recipe. My own recipe is a lighter version made with whole blueberries rather than blueberry juice and with the addition of the rind and juice of a lemon.

20 fresh or frozen
  blueberries
zest and freshly
  squeezed juice
  of ¼ lemon
about 500 ml/2 cups
  Unflavoured
  Kombucha (page
  20), to top up

1 x 500-ml/17-oz.
  capacity glass bottle
  with airtight lid

MAKES 1 BOTTLE
AND SERVES 2–4

Add the lemon zest and juice and the blueberries to the bottle. If using fresh blueberries, squash them gently before adding to the bottle so the lovely blue colour is released into the kombucha. Top up with unflavoured kombucha leaving a 1-cm/⅜-inch air space at the top, then seal tightly.

Leave the sealed bottle at room temperature, out of direct sunlight, for 2–3 days before testing for carbonation (see page 17), then refrigerate. Serve cold.

BLUEBERRIES are high in vitamin C, antioxidants (for fighting cancer-causing free radicals) and anthocyanins (giving the blue colour to the berries) for heart health. They also help to fight urinary tract infections and have proved effective in boosting memory and brain health in recent studies.

PASSION FRUIT & VANILLA TEA

This recipe has been contributed by the Berlin Kombucha Society, who started their business in 2015 and have since opened a thriving vegan restaurant in Berlin called the Black Sheep Café. We have swapped brewing tips since the beginning and they have a been a valuable resource for me, as well as others, offering regular workshops for kombucha-making at their premises.

'We made this kombucha on the spur of the moment when a customer gifted us 30 passion fruits. They were so ripe and smelt delicious, so we had to kombucha them! The result was a refreshing and summery kombucha, perfect for when passion fruit is in season.'

Cut each passion fruit in half and scoop out the insides (seeds and pulp) with a teaspoon, dropping them straight into a large brewing jar.

Slice the piece of vanilla pod/bean in half and scrape a teaspoon down the middle to remove the seeds. Add the seeds and pod/bean to the jar.

Pour over the unflavoured kombucha and stir well to thoroughly combine. Seal and leave at room temperature for 24 hours to allow the flavours to infuse.

Put a measuring jug/pitcher in the sink and position a fine-mesh sieve or strainer over the top. Carefully pour the passion fruit kombucha through the strainer to remove the passion fruit seeds and vanilla pod/bean.

Decant into bottles, leaving a 1-cm/⅜-inch air space at the top then seal.

Leave the sealed bottles at room temperature, out of direct sunlight, for 2–3 days before testing for carbonation (see page 17), then refrigerate.

Serve cold.

5 fresh, ripe passion fruits
¼ vanilla pod/bean (about 2.5 cm/1 inch)
about 2 litres/2 quarts plus ½ cup Unflavoured Kombucha (page 20), to top up

a large glass brewing jar with airtight lid
4 x 500-ml/17-oz. capacity glass bottles with airtight lids

MAKES 4 BOTTLES AND SERVES 8-16

BASE OF
VEGETABLE

SOUR RHUBARB FIZZ

Rhubarb is a classic English vegetable and one of my absolute favourite flavours with its natural tang enhancing the sour sweetness of the kombucha. It is also the first thing to come up in the spring and the first thing you start to see at farmers' markets, so if it's not in your garden it will be in your neighbours'. I use a light green tea base for this recipe as it allows the subtle rhubarb to come through, complemented by the sour apple to give it bite.

2 green apples (such as Granny Smith)
2 litres/2 quarts plus ½ cup Unflavoured Kombucha (page 20)

RHUBARB SYRUP
500 g/1 lb. 2 oz. red rhubarb or forced rhubarb
100 g/½ cup granulated/white sugar, to taste

a cold-press juicer
4 x 500-ml/17-oz. capacity glass bottles with airtight lids

MAKES 4 BOTTLES
AND SERVES 8-16

To make the rhubarb syrup, top and tail the rhubarb stalks, chop up finely and cover with 500 ml/2 cups of water in a saucepan. Bring to the boil over medium heat. Reduce to a simmer leaving on low–medium heat for 20 minutes until the rhubarb has broken down and lost most of its pink colouring, gently removing any foam as it appears. Strain the liquid into a separate pan without squashing the rhubarb, and bring to the boil once again. Add the sugar to taste – you can add as little or as much as you like here; it is really personal preference on how sweet you would like your syrup. Once boiled, reduce the heat and leave to simmer for another 20 minutes, reducing the liquid to a thick, syrupy consistency. Leave to cool completely, bottle and refrigerate.

Once cold, juice the apples in the cold-press juicer, and add roughly 50 ml/3½ tablespoons of the rhubarb syrup and one-quarter of the apple juice to each bottle. Top up with unflavoured kombucha leaving a 1-cm/⅜-inch air space at the top then seal tightly.

Leave the sealed bottles at room temperature, out of direct sunlight, for 1–2 days before testing for carbonation (see page 17). Due to the sugar content in the syrup, it is advisable to check your rhubarb kombucha after 2 days to see how much fizz has built up. Refrigerate when the taste and fizz are to your liking. Serve cold.

RHUBARB STALKS
contain complex
B-vitamins such as
folates, riboflavin,
niacin, vitamin B6
(pyridoxine), thiamin
and pantothenic acid.
Rhubarb also aids
digestion, is rich in
vitamin K (helping to
prevent Alzheimer's
disease) and promotes
bone health. It is full
of antioxidants and
is believed to reduce
the risk of
cardiovascular
problems.

VIRGIN MARY

I like my Virgin Mary spicy, so I tend to be quite generous with the
Worcestershire and Tabasco sauces. I advise you to taste as you go
along to get the proportions right for you, so I have specified a fairly
wide range of quantities on the spices. The kombucha here
is your vodka substitute, and while it does not taste like vodka, the
vinegary tones enhance the tomato juice and spices no end. This is
a wonderful alternative to alcohol as an aperitif or a Sunday morning
pick-me-up.

100 ml/⅓ cup
    good-quality tomato
    juice with low
    sodium content
½–1 teaspoon
    Worcestershire
    sauce (I use Lea &
    Perrins®)
5–10 drops of
    Tabasco® sauce
½ teaspoon
    horseradish sauce

a pinch of salt
2 grinds of black
    pepper, plus extra
    to serve
100 ml/⅓ cup
    Unflavoured
    Kombucha (page 20)

TO SERVE
ice cubes
1 celery stick/rib
a wedge of lime

SERVES 1

Mix the tomato juice, Worcestershire sauce,
Tabasco, horseradish, salt and pepper together in
a jug/pitcher (or glass jar with a lid, given a good
shake) before adding the unflavoured kombucha.

Stir again before pouring over ice with an
additional grind of pepper, a celery stick/rib
and a wedge of lime.

STRIPED CANDY BEETROOT/ BEET & LIME TEA

Pretty pink candy-striped beetroot/beets are a staple at our farmers' market, and we usually choose the little ones as they tend to be sweeter.

The earthy flavour of the beetroot/beet is balanced by the sweet, sharp apple and the addition of the lime. The beetroots/beets should be firm to the touch. If they are soft, then they will yield less juice with a more bitter flavour.

I love to drink this as a fresh juice when the time-sensitive vitamins of the vegetable are at their peak.

4 baby candy beetroots/beets
1 apple
zest and freshly squeezed juice of ½ lime
about 500 ml/2 cups Unflavoured Kombucha (page 20), to top up

a cold-press juicer
1 x 500-ml/17-oz. capacity glass bottle with airtight lid

MAKES 1 BOTTLE AND SERVES 2-4

Juice the beetroots/beets and apple together in the cold-press juicer. It should yield around 200 ml/¾ cup of juice. Pour into the bottle and add the lime zest (if desired) and juice. Top up with unflavoured kombucha leaving a 1-cm/ ⅜-inch air space at the top, then seal tightly.

Refrigerate to chill and consume immediately or within 3 days. If you prefer not to add the lime zest to the bottle, you could sprinkle it as a decoration before serving.

CHILLI/CHILE & PINEAPPLE KOMBUCHA

I met Shirley and Elizabeth early in 2015, soon after we both started our micro-breweries. Kombucha was still relatively unknown in the UK at this time and finding others with the same passion for the subject, who were experiencing the same challenges of turning the live brew into a business, was hugely comforting for me.

At Thirsty House Kombucha, they believe that every live organism responds to its environment. As such their aim is to create a harmonious and passionate environment for the kombucha, because it too is alive. Everyone who visits produces their own unique kombucha batch, which makes it a rich and satisfying experience. Not only will the kombucha base and flavourings influence how your kombucha tastes, you too will add your personal uniqueness to it!

When asked to contribute to this book, they said, 'Once we realised that kombucha had limitless flavouring potential, we started experimenting with fresh and seasonal fruits, vegetables and herbs that were available to us at the time. One of the first kombucha experiences and most exciting flavours we produced was a combination of chilli/chile and pineapple.

'Our chilli/chile plant grew well during the summer months. Lots of flowers magically turned into an abundance of beautiful, vivid red chillies/chiles. Too many to share with our curry-loving friends, so to make the most of our fresh red chillies/chiles and curious to find out what 'drinking' them would be like, we set about experimenting with all sorts of flavour combinations. This one won hands down.

'We hope you enjoy this combination as much as we do! Just a note of caution: let your taste buds as well as your tolerance for a bit of heat and spice guide you.'

a few 2-cm/¾-inch rings of ripe pineapple, cut into chunks

1 ripe red chilli/chile, sliced into extra-fine rings

3 litres/3 quarts plus ¾ cup Unflavoured Kombucha (page 20)

6 x 500-ml/17-oz. capacity glass bottle with airtight lid

MAKES 6 BOTTLES AND SERVES 12–24

Put 1–3 chunks of pineapple and 1–3 slices of chilli/chile into each bottle and top up with unflavoured kombucha leaving a 1-cm/⅜-inch air space at the top, then seal tightly.

Leave the sealed bottles at room temperature, out of direct sunlight, for 1–2 days before testing for carbonation (see page 17). Refrigerate when the taste and fizz are to your liking. Serve cold.

FENNEL's 'anise' flavour is known to provide relief for indigestion, flatulence, anaemia, heart disease and high blood pressure. It is also believed to inhibit cancer tumours, relieve colic, boost the immune system and help with respiratory disorders.

FENNEL & APPLE KOMBUCHA

Vegetable kombucha is notoriously difficult to perfect. The flavour of fresh vegetables, unlike fruit, changes dramatically with fermentation. They can sometimes go bitter, become overpowering or just taste simply not right. For this reason, I have only one suggestion: experiment, experiment, experiment!

The pro fermenters over at the Cultured Pickle Shop in Berkeley, California, USA, are doing just this; no holds barred experimentation. Their results, a mélange of flavours, are an inspiration to all of us in the world of fermentation. If you like this recipe, I recommend you look into their wonderful creations on their website (see Resources, page 94).

My own version of fennel and apple kombucha is only for the more discerning of kombucha drinkers. This recipe produces a sweet juice at first turning to a slightly bitter tonic over a period of a few days. The flavour is not too sweet – there is just enough earth with a touch of sour lime. Hopefully this will serve to inspire you to create more vegetable concoctions.

As with the other vegetable recipes, I believe it is best consumed immediately or within a few days of bottling.

1 fennel bulb
1 large apple
freshly squeezed juice
    of ½ lime
about 300 ml/1¼ cups
    Unflavoured
    Kombucha (page
    20), to top up

a cold-press juicer
1 x 500-ml/17-oz.
    capacity glass bottle
    with airtight lid

MAKES 1 BOTTLE
AND SERVES 2-4

Juice the fennel and apple together in the cold-press juicer. It should yield around 200 ml/¾ cup of juice. Add the lime juice and pour into the bottle. Top up with unflavoured kombucha, leaving a 1-cm/⅜-inch air space at the top, then seal tightly. Refrigerate and consume once chilled or within 3 days. Serve cold.

BASE OF
FLOWER

ROSE PETAL TEA

Roses have long been used in Middle Eastern cooking, although my most vivid associations of roses with food are of receiving very sweet rose-flavoured Turkish delight every Christmas.

Rosebuds and rose petals create a delicate, fragrant kombucha which feels like a luxurious treat. You can purchase edible rose petals online or from specialist health food shops. I actually like the intensity of the dried buds, but you can also pick roses from your garden and use them in cooking or brewing as long as they have not been exposed to chemicals or fertilizers.

ROSEBUDS & PETALS have a long tradition of being used as a herbal sedative, as an anti-depressant and are often used as an anti-inflammatory.

2 teaspoons dried rosebuds, 4 teaspoons fresh rose petals or 1 teaspoon rosewater
about 500 ml/2 cups Unflavoured Kombucha (page 20), to top up

1 x 500-ml/17-oz. capacity glass bottle with airtight lid

MAKES 1 BOTTLE
AND SERVES 2-4

Put the rosebuds, rose petals or rosewater into the bottle and top up with kombucha leaving a 1-cm/³⁄₈-inch air space at the top, then seal tightly.

Leave the sealed bottle at room temperature, out of direct sunlight, for 3 days before testing for carbonation (see page 17). Refrigerate when the taste and fizz are to your liking. Serve cold.

NOTE A wonderful alternative to rose petals is cherry blossom, which is available in the early spring.

LAVENDER LOVE

Black tea kombucha works very well with lavender. We often think of lavender in terms of aromatherapy and scented relaxants, but this pale greyish-purple flower has culinary uses, too, as a subtle perfume in sweet foods, baked goods and chocolate. Lavender is used a herbal remedy for relieving anxiety and inducing peaceful sleep. Historically paired with black, green and herbal teas, it is a natural accompaniment for kombucha.

When picking lavender flowers, ensure they have not been treated with pesticides. We maintain two or three lavender plants and when the season finishes, we cut off the buds and dry them by hanging them upside down in the kitchen so there's always a supply of home-grown lavender.

1 large or 2 small lavender buds about 500 ml/2 cups Unflavoured Kombucha (page 20), to top up

1 x 500-ml/17-oz. capacity glass bottle with airtight lid

MAKES 1 BOTTLE AND SERVES 2–4

Put the lavender buds in the bottle and top up with unflavoured kombucha leaving a 1-cm/ ⅜-inch air space at the top then seal tightly.

Leave the sealed bottle at room temperature, out of direct sunlight, for 2–3 days. Taste daily and remove the lavender when the kombucha is perfumed enough for your liking. Test for carbonation (see page 17) and refrigerate when the taste and fizz are to your liking. Serve cold.

NOTE This may well take more than 3 days to gain carbonation, because flowers do not contain the same amount of sugars as fruits and vegetables – be patient.

HOPPY PALE ALE

I was given the idea for this recipe when I was visiting the fantastic microbrewery Katalyst Kombucha in Greenfield, Massachusetts, USA. One of the brewers comes from a beer-making background and had applied his knowledge of hops to their kombucha. I do not drink alcohol very much anymore but still love the taste of really good hoppy beer. Katalyst have created a wonderful version of a non-alcoholic India pale ale, with floral citrus notes; it's a sure-fire winner in converting beer drinkers to kombucha. I also add lemon juice to this recipe as I find it complements the hops.

Hops are a natural preservative and were originally added directly to beer barrels after fermentation was complete, to keep it fresh during transportation. The flower of the vine is what's used for flavouring. They've been grown in Britain commercially for more than 500 years, and there are so many different varieties, with some deeply bitter and others pleasantly akin to blackcurrant.

2–3 fresh hop flowers
freshly squeezed juice of
½ lemon
about 500 ml/2 cups
Unflavoured Kombucha
(page 20), to top up

1 x 500-ml/17-oz. capacity glass bottle with airtight lid

MAKES 1 BOTTLE
AND SERVES 2–4

Put the hop flowers into the bottle with the lemon juice, top up with unflavoured kombucha leaving a 1-cm/⅜-inch air space at the top, then seal tightly.

Leave the sealed bottle at room temperature, out of direct sunlight, for 24 hours before removing the hops. The hops have a strong flavour of their own and the oils will be drawn out naturally by the acidic kombucha in a very short period. If after 24 hours, you think that the hops flavour should be stronger, then steep for another day.

Leave for another 4 days before testing for carbonation (see page 17). Refrigerate when the taste and fizz are to your liking. Hops naturally slow down the carbonation by controlling the yeast, so these bottles will take longer to get fizzy than other brews. Serve cold.

FRESH HOPS can be found in British hedgerows in late summer and early autumn/fall. If you are unable to pick the flowers from the creeping vines, brewing shops (see Resources, page 94) sell a large variety of fresh hops in bags available in small quantities. My personal favourite variety is an American hop called 'Citra', which I buy around the corner in Netil Market in Hackney, London. They can also be bought from most online brew shops. Fresh hops are best stored in the freezer – they will last a long time as you only need a few flowers per brew. Hops are also used as a natural medicine to treat insomnia and anxiety, so there's nothing to stop you from giving this drink a whirl.

HIBISCUS TEA

Hibiscus is a dark red late-blooming flower with a slight lemony flavour and a multitude of medicinal properties (see right). Growing in a range of colours including white, pink, purple and orange, it is the red flowers that are used as flavouring and for herbal remedies. Although most commonly consumed as a tea, the flower petals are used whole in cakes, incorporated into salads and are even cooked and eaten like spinach in China. Hibiscus is a popular flavour for kombucha, featuring as a standard in many commercial brands. This is not surprising, as a very small quantity delivers lots of taste and beautiful colouring as well as a boost for health.

6–8 dried hibiscus flowers
about 500 ml/2 cups
   Unflavoured Kombucha
   (page 20), to top up

1 x 500-ml/17-oz. capacity glass
  bottle with airtight lid

MAKES 1 BOTTLE
AND SERVES 2–4

Put the hibiscus flowers into the bottle and top up with unflavoured kombucha leaving a 1-cm/⅜-inch air space at the top, then seal tightly.

Watch the colour change rapidly as the day progresses and leave the sealed bottle at room temperature, out of direct sunlight, for 2–3 days before testing for carbonation (see page 17). Refrigerate when the taste and fizz are to your liking. Strain and serve cold.

NOTE Strawberries also work well with the flavour of hibiscus – for a variation add 4 large or 8 small strawberry halves to the bottle before topping up with unflavoured kombucha.

HIBISCUS FLOWERS help to lower blood pressure, prevent colds and flu, and are beneficial for weight loss, reducing anxiety and depression, and aiding digestion. They also act as a diuretic, lower levels of bad LDL cholesterol, protect the liver against infections and disease, and can provide relief from cramps and menstrual pain.

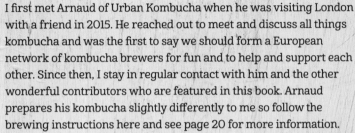

ELDERFLOWER & APRICOT KOMBUCHA

I first met Arnaud of Urban Kombucha when he was visiting London with a friend in 2015. He reached out to meet and discuss all things kombucha and was the first to say we should form a European network of kombucha brewers for fun and to help and support each other. Since then, I stay in regular contact with him and the other wonderful contributors who are featured in this book. Arnaud prepares his kombucha slightly differently to me so follow the brewing instructions here and see page 20 for more information.

When asked to contribute to this book, Arnaud said, 'I had the privilege to grow up in Western Switzerland, a region surrounded with beautiful lakes and majestic mountains. The abundance of sun in Alpine valleys makes for perfect conditions to grow a variety of fruits and herbs, and quite naturally Urban Kombucha's inspiration is deeply rooted in this idyllic land.

'This recipe is our tribute to the Valais region (think Swiss mountains, Swiss cheese and great landscapes). It is well known for its apricot and apple orchards. This is also where our kombucha brewery is located, with direct access to pristine, clear Alpine spring water. Elderflower grows nearby, and it is the flower of the elderberry bush that gives a light honey-like taste when infused.

'This elderflower and apricot kombucha is a light and refreshing beverage, so we like to use white tea as a base, but it goes without saying that we encourage people to experiment and see what fits.'

2 teaspoons white loose-leaf tea
3 teaspoons dried elderflowers
160 g/¾ cup raw evaporated
   cane sugar
1 SCOBY
100–200 ml/⅓–½ cup
   Unflavoured Kombucha (page
   20) or 30 ml/2 tablespoons
   distilled white vinegar
6 apricots, stoned/pitted and
   quartered or puréed

a 2.5-litre/3-quart capacity
   heatproof brewing jar
a tea ball
4 x 500-ml/17-oz. capacity glass
   bottles with airtight lids

MAKES 4 BOTTLES
AND SERVES 8–16

To prepare the base kombucha, boil 2 litres/ 2 quarts plus ½ cup of water in a stainless steel saucepan. Cool the water to a temperature of about 75°C (170°F) in the brewing jar before steeping the white tea with the elderflowers for 5 minutes. Sweeten with the sugar and cool to room temperature, then add the SCOBY and kombucha. Cover the jar with a piece of close-weave cotton and secure with an elastic band. Set aside for at least 7 and up to 10 days.

When the kombucha is ready for second fermentation, divide the apricot quarters between the bottles. Alternatively, purée a small portion of the apricots and mix with the apricot pieces for a slightly sweeter kombucha with richer mouthfeel.

Top up with the base kombucha leaving a 1-cm/ ⅜-inch air space at the top, then seal tightly.

Leave the sealed bottles at room temperature, out of direct sunlight, for 2 days before testing for carbonation (see page 17). Adding apricot will help carbonate the drink as it adds a small amount of sugar, so watch carefully as it evolves. Refrigerate for a further 5 days when the taste and fizz are to your liking.

Once the kombucha is properly infused with apricot taste, you can either leave the fruits in if you intend to drink your kombucha within a week or two, or you can take them out if you want to keep it for longer.

NOTE Send us a picture of your brew (see Resources, page 94) to get a postcard in return!

BASE OF
HERB, SPICE
& TEA

LEMONGRASS
KOMBUCHA

This delicately perfumed, Champagne-like kombucha is one of my absolute favourites. Use a light green tea for the Unflavoured Kombucha – it really allows the lemongrass to come through. In the early days of the business, a friend who is a wonderful chef suggested I start experimenting with lemongrass and the result is delicious! Lemongrass also works well paired with ginger or cardamom if you want to continue experimenting.

1 large or 2 small lemongrass stalks, plus extra to serve
about 500 ml/2 cups Unflavoured Kombucha (page 20), to top up

1 x 500-ml/17-oz. capacity glass bottle with airtight lid

MAKES 1 BOTTLE AND SERVES 2–4

Cut off both ends of the lemongrass and peel to remove the tough outer skin. Finely chop the inner stem or pop into a blender and blitz for a minute or two until you have a fine paste. (The reason for blending is to create more surface area for the kombucha to draw flavour and goodness from.) Put this in the bottle and top up with unflavoured kombucha leaving a 1-cm/⅜-inch air space at the top, then seal tightly.

Leave the sealed bottle at room temperature, out of direct sunlight, for 2 days before testing for carbonation (see page 17). Refrigerate when the taste and fizz are to your liking.

You can strain the lemongrass away or leave it in. Serve cold with a stalk of fresh lemongrass and a straw to stir with.

LEMONGRASS helps with digestive ailments such as diarrhoea and constipation, and it has antibacterial and antifungal properties, which fight colds and flu. Lemongrass also helps to regulate cholesterol levels, is a cleanser and detoxifier, has anti-inflammatory properties which help with arthritis, helps fight depression and low mood and is used as an ingredient to reduce body odour!

APPLE & MINT COOLER

This is one of the recipes I enjoy making the most. The combination of green apple and mint tastes clean, clear and refreshing. I use Granny Smiths from time to time; however they are often grown on a very large industrial scale, so I prefer to find a sour, crisp local apple in the autumn/fall, like Braeburn or Cox's.

1 large apple or 150 ml/
⅔ cup fresh apple
juice
4 large or 5 small fresh
mint leaves
about 500 ml/2 cups
Unflavoured
Kombucha (page 20),
to top up

*a cold-press juicer
(optional)*
*1 x 500-ml/17-oz.
capacity glass bottle
with airtight lid*

MAKES 1 BOTTLE
AND SERVES 2–4

If using a large fresh apple, juice it in the cold-press juicer. It should yield around 150 ml/⅔ cup of juice. If this is not possible, there are now a wonderful range of cloudy farm-apple juices available on the market distinguished by variety. Some are mixed with ginger, which will also be a tasty addition to your brew.

Pour the apple juice into the bottle, add the mint leaves, top up with unflavoured kombucha leaving a 1-cm/⅜-inch air space at the top, then seal tightly.

Leave the sealed bottle at room temperature, out of direct sunlight, for 2 days before testing for carbonation (see page 17). Strain away the mint leaves if desired and refrigerate when the taste and fizz are to your liking.

When ready to serve, pour into a jug/pitcher filled with ice. Add fizzy water to turn it into a refreshing spritz and enjoy.

NOTE You can use lime instead of mint for a zingy variation of this cooler.

LYCHEE BASIL MOJITO

A close friend first surprised me with fresh lychees by bringing an entire crate, procured from a local Turkish greengrocer, to a dinner party. Until then, I had only ever eaten the canned version, delicious in their own right, but packed in a sweet syrup. Lychees come from South-east Asia and Brazil. Since then we have bought them regularly in winter when they are tastiest. A ripe lychee is easily peeled and by cutting down one side, you can squeeze out the large stone/pit with your finger.

3 lychees, peeled, stoned/pitted and stalks removed
2 large fresh basil leaves, washed and dried
about 500 ml/2 cups Unflavoured Kombucha (page 20), to top up

TO SERVE
ice cubes
1–2 sprigs of fresh mint

1 x 500-ml/17-oz. capacity glass bottle with airtight lid

MAKES 1 BOTTLE AND SERVES 2–4

Put the lychees into the bottle along with the washed basil leaves and top up with unflavoured kombucha leaving a 1-cm/3⁄8-inch air space at the top, then seal tightly.

Leave the sealed bottle at room temperature, out of direct sunlight, for 2 days before testing for carbonation (see page 17). Refrigerate when the taste and fizz are to your liking.

You can strain the fruit and herbs out or leave them in. Serve over ice garnished with a sprig of fresh mint.

NOTE I like to drink this when it is 1 week old after the subtle lychee and basil flavours have combined nicely in the bottle. The lychee sweetness will boost carbonation so drink it within a month.

LYCHEES support weight loss, promote blood circulation, strengthen the immune system and maintain blood pressure and fluid balance. They are also a natural diuretic and improve digestion. A member of the soapberry family, this sweet, fragrant fruit is a wonderful source of fibre, antioxidants and vitamins – an especially good source of vitamin C containing a third more vitamin C per 100 g/3½ oz. than an orange.

GINGER & LEMON FIZZ

This is a favourite of so many kombucha brewers and drinkers. Almost every commercial kombucha company creates their own version of this recipe. At home, it is my go-to, tastes-great recipe. It can be hard to get wrong and you can make it a mild subtle ginger elixir or a bold fiery tonic.

Ginger helps kombucha to get fizzy. It contains natural lactobacillus bacteria that eats the sugar, creating CO_2 (or 'fizz'). Ginger can be added to other recipes in varying amounts for precisely that purpose. Combined with lemon, this brew is a healthy take on the classic ginger beer. It gets fizzy quickly which is infinitely satisfying and produces a brew with a complex flavour profile.

Ginger and lemon lends itself well to the flavour of black tea as well as green tea, so go with your preference.

1 tablespoon freshly juiced ginger or 1 tablespoon grated fresh ginger
freshly squeezed juice of ½ lemon
about 500 ml/2 cups Unflavoured Kombucha (page 20), to top up

a cold-press juicer (optional)
1 x 500-ml/17-oz. capacity glass bottle with airtight lid

MAKES 1 BOTTLE
AND SERVES 2–4

Simply add the ginger juice or grated ginger and lemon juice to the bottle, top up with unflavoured kombucha leaving a 1-cm/⅜-inch air space at the top, then seal tightly.

Leave the sealed bottle at room temperature, out of direct sunlight, for 2–3 days before testing for carbonation (see page 17). Refrigerate when the taste and fizz are to your liking. Strain if desired and serve cold.

NOTE Use this as a medicinal tonic when you have a sick tummy, as a hangover aid and as a cold-busting, immune system-boosting, delicious-tasting drink.

TURMERIC IMMUNE BOOST

Turmeric, that golden yellow spice used as a base for curries and in South-east Asian cuisine, is a pleasantly surprising flavour with which to make kombucha. Turmeric is very on-trend in London at the moment, which is understandable considering the centuries-old belief in its healing properties. I have sampled turmeric crackers, chocolates and cashew milk lattes, and so finally tried a brew of my own. Turmeric is such a light flavour; peppery, flowery. It is also a little bit like nasturtiums, the edible flower found in salads, and the second version works particularly well with a bit of honey to balance out the dry flavours, speed up the carbonation process and to make a deliciously refreshing medicinal tonic.

VERSION 1:
A LIGHT FRESH TONIC
**1 light pinch
(1/16 teaspoon)
ground turmeric
freshly squeezed juice
of ½ lemon
about 500 ml/2 cups
Unflavoured
Kombucha (page
20), to top up**

VERSION 2:
A SUPER-CHARGED
MEDICINE
**1 hearty pinch
(⅛ teaspoon)
ground turmeric
freshly squeezed juice
of ½ lemon
½ teaspoon honey
about 500 ml/2 cups
Unflavoured
Kombucha (page
20), to top up**

*1 x 500-ml/17-oz.
capacity glass bottle
with airtight lid*

MAKES 1 BOTTLE
AND SERVES 2-4

Add the turmeric, lemon juice and honey
(if making Version 2) to the bottle and top up
with unflavoured kombucha leaving a 1-cm/
⅜-inch air space at the top. Seal tightly.

Leave the sealed bottle at room temperature, out
of direct sunlight, for 1–2 days before testing for
carbonation (see page 17). Refrigerate when the
taste and fizz are to your liking. Serve cold.

TURMERIC is commonly known to assist in digestion and to
strengthen the liver. The antioxidant and anti-inflammatory
properties of curcumin (a compound which gives turmeric
is bright orange hue) have also been linked to the reduction
of heart attacks, in the delay of diabetes and to curb joint pain.

PLUM & THYME TEA

I keep this as a seasonal kombucha, and pick the plums in late summer, when my mother has an excess from her fruit orchards, or when the farmers' markets are over-spilling with deep purple, red and yellow varietals.

Any plums work for this recipe, but I particularly like the black damsons due to the pretty hue they give to the kombucha. Golden plums work well too and I instinctively go for the juicy ones. My mother grows Victoria plums alongside the apples in her orchard, which are very sour and also create a gratifying tonic. The thyme adds a fragrant base to the subtle perfume of the plum. My boyfriend compares a sour plum kombucha to a Belgian lambic beer and he, in contrast to me, likes to seek out the hardest greenest plums for our secondary ferment.

1 large black plum or 2 small damson plums
1 sprig of fresh thyme
about 500 ml/2 cups Unflavoured Kombucha (page 20), to top up

1 x 500-ml/17-oz. capacity glass bottle with airtight lid

MAKES 1 BOTTLE
AND SERVES 2–4

Slice the plum or plums into thin wedges, carefully removing the stone/pit, and put them into the bottle along with a sprig of thyme. Top up with unflavoured kombucha leaving a 1-cm/⅜-inch air space at the top, then seal tightly.

Leave the sealed bottle at room temperature, out of direct sunlight, for 2 days before testing for carbonation (see page 17). When the taste and fizz are to your liking, strain the liquid if desired and return to the bottle.

Refrigerate and serve cold.

NOTE For a sweeter variation of this recipe, scrape the seeds from ½ vanilla pod/bean into the bottle instead of the thyme.

JASMINE KOMBUCHA

Jasmine green tea will create a lightly perfumed kombucha, which has such a delicate flavour that it needs no further additions. Treat this as you would the Unflavoured Kombucha recipe on page 20, but using jasmine green tea. This needs a shorter first ferment, because after a number of weeks you will find it hard to distinguish the jasmine as the vinegary flavour of the kombucha will overpower it.

2–3 teaspoons jasmine green loose-leaf tea or 6 jasmine teabags

160 g/¾ cup caster/granulated sugar, plus extra to bottle

1 SCOBY

125–200 ml/½–¾ cup Unflavoured Kombucha (page 20) or 30 ml/2 tablespoons distilled white vinegar

a handful of (dark) raisins (optional)

a 2.5-litre/3-quart capacity heatproof brewing jar, sterilized

a tea ball (optional)

a close-weave cotton cloth

4 x 500-ml/17-oz. capacity glass bottles with airtight lids

MAKES 4 BOTTLES
AND SERVES 8-16

Bring 2 litres/2 quarts plus ½ cup of water to the boil in a stainless-steel pan. Leave the water in the pan or transfer to the heatproof brewing jar. Cool the water to around 75°C (170°F) and, if using loose-leaf tea, put it in the tea ball, and steep the tea for 2–4 minutes depending on how strong you like the flavour.

Remove the tea ball or bags and using a wooden spoon, stir the sugar into the still-warm steeped tea to dissolve. Allow to cool completely to room temperature: 22°C (72°F) or less.

Add the unflavoured kombucha or vinegar and with clean hands, gently lower the SCOBY into the cooled, sweetened tea with the paler side facing upwards and any yeasty strands facing towards the bottom. Cover the jar with a close-weave cotton cloth (see page 14) and secure with an elastic band. Set aside at room temperature, out of direct sunlight, for at least 7 days.

Taste daily and, when the jasmine flavour is to your liking, bottle the kombucha leaving a 1-cm/⅜-inch air space at the top, then seal tightly.

Leave the sealed bottles at room temperature, out of direct sunlight, for 2 days before testing for carbonation (see page 17). This might take a while to carbonate depending on the sugar left in the brew, so add ½ teaspoon per bottle, or a few (dark) raisins to give it a little extra fizz if necessary. Refrigerate and serve cold.

BLACK MOONLIGHT

One of the master brewers of kombucha who specialise in flavouring their kombucha in the primary ferment using specific teas is KBBK (Kombucha Brooklyn), founded by husband and wife team Eric and Jessica Childs. They have kindly contributed two of their exquisite recipes here. Use either the Black Moonlight or White Dragon ingredients, not both.

Of these recipes, they say, 'When thinking about flavoring your kombucha, one should look to the heart and history of beverage fermentation, where ingredients are chosen, fermented and consumed. For example, a winemaker will carefully select their grapes to make the best wine. As a kombucha-maker, you have the same ability. By choosing the right tea or tea blends, one can make a complex delux brew.

'At KBBK it is our primary way of teaching others to flavour their kombucha. Here are two blends that we love.'

240 ml/1 cup cane sugar, for primary fermentation
240 ml/1 cup Unflavoured Kombucha (page 20)
1 SCOBY
40 ml/⅓ cup cane sugar, for bottle conditioning

BLACK MOONLIGHT
12 g/½ oz. imperial pu-erh loose-leaf tea
12 g/½ oz. white peony loose-leaf tea

(continued opposite)

Steep the imperial pu-erh tea (or half of the silver needle and all of the dragonwell tea together if making White Dragon kombucha) in 950 ml/1 quart of boiling water for 20 minutes. Add the cane sugar for primary fermentation and stir with a wooden spoon to dissolve. Allow to cool to room temperature: 26°C (79°F) or less.

Add the unflavoured kombucha and, with clean hands, lower the SCOBY into the cooled tea,

WHITE DRAGON (VARIATION)

12 g/½ oz. silver needle white loose-leaf tea

6 g/¼ oz. dragonwell loose-leaf tea

a 2.5-litre/3-quart capacity heatproof brewing jar, sterilized

a tea ball

a close-weave cotton cloth

4 x 500-ml/17-oz. capacity glass bottles with airtight lids

MAKES 4 BOTTLES
AND SERVES 8–16

cover and set aside at room temperature, out of direct sunlight, for 16 days, but keep an eye on it.

After this primary fermentation, transfer the kombucha to a large brewing vessel.

Steep the white peony tea (or the remaining silver needle tea if making White Dragon kombucha) in 1.2 litres/1½ quarts of boiling water for 10 minutes. Add the cane sugar for conditioning, stir to dissolve and cool to room temperature. Add this sugared tea to the kombucha in the brewing vessel. Bottle leaving a 1-cm/⅜-inch air space at the top, then seal tightly.

Leave the sealed bottles at room temperature, out of direct sunlight, for 2 weeks, testing for carbonation and 'burping' (see page 17) every day or so. Refrigerate and serve cold.

INDEX

RESOURCES

KOMBUCHA PRODUCERS

Berlin Kombucha Society
www.blacksheepberlin.com
*Kombucha producers operating
from vegan café, Black Sheep.*

GT's Synergy®
www.synergydrinks.com
*California-based producer
of kombucha energy drinks.*

Katalyst Kombucha
www.katalystkombucha.com
*Commercial producer of
kombucha in Greenfield,
Massachusetts, USA. Available
across North America.*

KBBK (Kombucha Brooklyn)
www.kombuchabrooklyn.com
*Suppliers of kombucha cultures,
brewing kits and equipment, with
a wealth of information online
and in their book: Kombucha!
(Avery, Penguin Group, 2013)*

L.A Brewery
www.labrewery.co.uk
*Louise Avery's kombucha
micro-brewery based in Suffolk.*

Thirsty House Kombucha
www.thirstyhouse
kombucha.co.uk
*Brewer of organic and cold-
pressed kombucha based in
Streatham, London, UK.*

Urban Kombucha
www.urbankombucha.ch
Swiss organic kombucha brewer.

INGREDIENTS

Adagio Teas
www.adagiotea.co.uk
www.adagio.com
*UK and US supplier of loose-leaf
and specialist teas.*

Borough Market
www.boroughmarket.org.uk
*London's most renowned food
market.*

Cultured®
www.culturedpickleshop.com
*Supplier of fermented foods,
including sauerkraut, kimchi,
kombucha and other specialist
pickles, based in Berkeley,
California, USA.*

Cultures for Health™
www.culturesforhealth.com
*US stockist of pH strips,
non-leaded brewing vessels
and cultures, including SCOBYs.*

Eat My Flowers
www.eatmyflowers.co.uk
UK producer of edible flowers.

Fairtrade Foundation®
www.fairtrade.org.uk
*Useful resource for sourcing tea
and other ingredients ethically.*

Fine Food Specialist
www.finefoodspecialist.co.uk
*Online store for specialist
culinary ingredients, including
edible flowers.*

Fusion Teas
www.fusionteas.com
*Good-quality loose-leaf teas,
accessories and SCOBYs, shipped
across North America.*

JING™
www.jingtea.com
*Online store for teas as well as
brewing and serving equipment,
shipped worldwide.*

Netil Market
www.eatworkart.com
*Permanent market traders
daily, plus food on Saturdays
in Hackney, London, UK.*

Sous Chef
www.souschef.co.uk
*Fantastic online source of quality
ingredients (including edible
flowers) and cooking equipment.*

Teas Etc®
www.teasetc.com
*Purveyor of specialist teas with
US and international shipping.*

The Tea Exchange
www.londonteaexchange.co.uk
*Exquisite and ethical tea shop in
Spitalfields, London, UK, that
provides a wealth of extpertise
and supports small plantations,
producing quality, premium tea.*

Trader Joe's
www.traderjoes.com
US food store.

Waitrose
www.waitrose.com
UK supermarket with wide variety of fresh, frozen and dried produce.

Whole Foods Market
www.wholefoodsmarket.com
Fresh, good-quality food store.

EQUIPMENT

Amazon
www.amazon.co.uk
www.amazon.com
Everything from jars and bottles to filters, strainers and funnels.

Crate & Barrel
www.crateandbarrel.com
Fantastic source of housewares and kitchen accessories in the US.

Dunelm
www.dunelm.com
UK Homewares store selling Kilner brewing jars.

IKEA
www.ikea.com
Homewares superstore selling brewing vessels and flip-top bottles.

Lakeland
www.lakeland.co.uk
UK kitchenware store with good-quality, affordable equipment including brewing jars.

NISBETS®
www.nisbets.co.uk
UK professional kitchen supplier for bulk-buying coffee filters.

Wilkinson's
www.wilko.com
UK store selling flip-top bottles.

Williams-Sonoma
www.williams-sonoma.com
Cookshop with everything for home-brewing.

FURTHER READING

The Art of Fermentation *by Sandor Ellix Katz (Chelsea Green Publishing, 2012)*

Kombucha! *by Eric and Jessica Childs (Avery, Penguin Group, 2013)*

Kombucha, the Balancing Act *by Len Porzio (online)*

ACKNOWLEDGMENTS

A massive thank you to Ian, my partner.
To Jennifer Christie at Graham Maw Christie;
Cindy, Steph, Megan, Julia and Leslie at Ryland
Peters & Small; and the amazing photography
team: Clare, Jen and Rachel. And to my
contributers, KBBK, Thirsty House, Urban
Kombucha and Berlin Kombucha Society.

Senior designer Megan Smith
Commissioning editor Stephanie Milner
Production manager Gordana Simakovic
Creative director Leslie Harrington
Editorial director Julia Charles
Publisher Cindy Richards

Food stylist Rachel Wood
Prop stylist Jennifer Kay
Indexer Vanessa Bird

First published in 2016, reissued 2018.
This revised edition published in 2023
by Ryland Peters & Small
20–21 Jockey's Fields, London WC1R 4BW
and 341 E 116th St, New York NY 10029

www.rylandpeters.com

10 9 8 7 6 5 4 3 2 1

ISBN: 978-1-78879-476-3

Printed in China

A CIP record for this
book is available
from the British
Library.

US Library
of Congress
Cataloging-in-
Publication Data
has been applied for.

Notes

• Both British (Metric) and American (Imperial
plus US cups) measurements are included in
these recipes for your convenience, however it is
important to work with one set of measurements
and not alternate between the two within a
recipe. Liquid measurements listed in ounces
should be considered fluid ounces. All spoon
measurements are level unless specified.
• When a recipe calls for the grated zest of citrus
fruit, buy unwaxed fruit and wash well before
using. If you can only find treated fruit, scrub
well in warm soapy water before using.
• To sterilize brewing jars and bottles, wash them
in hot, soapy water and rinse in boiling water.
Sterilize the lids by boiling for 5 minutes or
according to the manufacturer's instructions.

Disclaimer

FSC
www.fsc.org

MIX
Paper from
responsible sources
FSC® C106563